MW01490942

PERSEVERED

CHOOSING YOUR BEST POSSIBLE DESTINY

BELINDA MENDEZ

ISBN 978-1-64140-036-7 (paperback)
ISBN 978-1-64140-037-4 (digital)

Christian Faith Publishing, Inc.
832 Park Avenue
Meadville, PA 16335
www.christianfaithpublishing.com

Printed in the United States of America

THANK YOU TO WALLY, EDWIN and the entire Kai of Jobos Beach crew for providing me with a wonderful atmosphere and great food while I plugged into the wall and wrote my book. You guys are awesome!

Thank you to my daughter Joy P. Vidal for believing in me. Mommy loves you.

CHAPTER 1

He Spoke to Me!

Hi. My name is Belle. The meaning of my name is *to be beautiful.* I try to be beautiful inside and out. I was born in Manhattan, New York, in 1971 and raised in Long Island. I'm a freckled face with light skin; wild, curly, blonde hair; and soft brown eyes.

My story begins in Long Island at the ripe age of fifteen. I was an early bloomer with the curves of a nineteen-year-old, which caused a bit of a challenge in handling the attention of boys and men!

I, like many of you, was taken to church by my parents when I would have rather been playing with makeup, on the phone with friends, or shopping at the local mall. The church my family and I attended was a non-denominational church with a lot of Italians but a wide diversity of people as well. This church called *Upper Room* was equipped with a school from kindergarten through twelfth grade located on the downstairs level of which both myself and my younger brother attended. This church housed over one thousand five hundred members on Sundays in the '80s but houses over five thousand today. The school was considered a Christian, private learning center that required students to wear uniforms.

It was on a humid August evening that I attended a teenage group meeting at the church to mingle, share, and learn with other teens. As I put on my jeans, summer blouse, and pink sneakers, I had no idea that my life was about to change forever.

A very mature man by the name of Mr. Jack Heinz was in charge of the teenage meetings and our teacher and mentor. Mr. Heinz is soft-spoken in his tone but sharp in his delivery of wisdom. He is a serious man that can be funny on occasion so he keeps the interest of the youth group.

As I walk into the classroom, I see that the room is packed with one seat left for me. I thought to myself, something special or really interesting must be taking place tonight because the room is full. Sure enough, Mr. Heinz pulls out a record player. For you youngsters reading this, a record player is a form of old-style CD player that played large vinyl discs of music.

Mr. Heinz begins questioning us about music, specifically rock and heavy metal. Freestyle music artists like Lisette Melendez, Taylor Dane, and Samantha Fox is what I was most familiar with. I knew who the rock group Kiss was and the Beetles, but rock was not my forte. I realized quickly that I did not have much knowledge on this subject to bring to the table.

As Mr. Heinz collects information from the teenage group, he then explains to us that certain types of music have hidden messages in the lyrics. He then explains that when certain records or vinyl music discs are played backward on the record player, the hidden messages are revealed. We, as a whole group, were all in awe. We were not prepared for what was about to happen next.

While Mr. Heinz did his best to give us all a heads up and caution us, we were speechless, in shock, frightened, and with chills going through us as we listened to the first song playing backward. There were satanic voices in the midst of demonic hurling voices and a rhythm so toe curling I'd rather forget. A snakelike voice with a hissing sound sang or rather screamed messages of killing yourself, killing others, and F bombs were everywhere.

Hearing the voices and the very clear messages made hell very real to me. The screams, agonizing moans of pain, harsh beats of music, and destructive messages such as "Give me your soul" were chilling to all of us. Matthew 13:50 of the King James version of the Bible describes hell as a fiery furnace where those who go will be wailing and gnashing their teeth. Hell does not sound like a resort to me.

Mr. Heinz continues his lesson expressing that these hidden messages are a way for Satan to brainwash and manipulate us into doing his will which is to steal, kill, and destroy according to John 10:10. Mr. Heinz played about four songs that night. First, forwards; then, backward. Each song was more terrifying than the previous in its hidden agenda. The purpose of the exposure to the music and its hidden messages was to bring awareness to us, as young people, and expose Satan for who he really is.

I left the meeting with my heart and spirit weighing heavily. How did God feel about His creation? How did He feel when His children are being misled and brainwashed by Satan through music? Who was Lucifer before he became Satan? Lucifer is one of the three archangels mentioned in the Bible. He was created by God to be the angel of worship, one whose ministry surrounded the heart of heaven. According to Ezekiel 28:13, he was an amazing being who was full of wisdom and perfect in beauty, adorned in diamonds, sapphires, onyx, and gold. Lucifer also had tambourines and multiple windpipes in him; meaning, he was a living, musical instrument. Mankind has only one windpipe.

As I sat in the car ride heading home with my parents and younger brother, Adam, I shared my lesson by Mr. Heinz with them. My heart became heavier as I shared my new-found knowledge with them.

That was Friday night and we were expecting family to visit us over the weekend. As soon as our minivan pulled into the driveway, Mom asked me to please clean the bathroom. I raced my little brother up the staircase and pulled out some Comet powder and a scrub brush and got busy cleaning.

Our bathroom was white and yellow, with a full tub, and large in size. I knelt down on the floor and began scrubbing the tub. All of a sudden, I became stiff and completely frozen. I was not able to talk. I tried to call Mom for help, but nothing came out of my mouth nor did my mouth even open.

Against the yellow-tiled walls appears guess who? Satan. I see before my very eyes Satan and God fighting over my soul. Satan had a very tight grip on my soul but God, being many times stronger, beat the mess out of Satan and left Him totally defeated. My soul was now safely in God's hands. Satan converted to a black spirit of death and he flew across the room as if he was desperately seeking a new soul to steal, kill, and destroy. God spoke directly to me saying, "Belle, what you have experienced here needs to be shared with others. There are classmates in your school that are listening to certain heavy metal and rock music artists. Listening to and corrupting of this music will change their hearts, minds, and destinies. Warn them that they must worship me for I am God. They need not worship another." God went on to say, "Anyone who continues to listen to this satanic music after hearing my warning may face death. Go, tell them. Warn them."

Okay, I know. I know, you're thinking to yourself, "What were you smoking that night Belle? How can I get some?" But things are about to get deeper, much deeper. You ain't heard nothing yet! I'm still kneeling on the bathroom floor, still frozen, unable to move. I think to myself, *Lord, how do I know you really want me to do this? Can you just confirm for me, God? Can you speak to Mrs. Mazzy, the classroom monitor at school, and confirm all this to her so then I'll know without a doubt that I'm not hallucinating, I'm not dreaming, and I really need to do this?*

I hear God tell me, "Yes." I then became unfrozen, able to move, and then took a moment to, by all means, adjust to the fact that God just spoke to me! God Himself thought it necessary to speak to me! Then I quickly got over myself while reminding myself that God also spoke through a donkey in Numbers 22:28. Okay, so God can speak to whomever He wants, through whomever He chooses, and whenever He chooses. But He chose me! I was imperfect. I was just a child still, but I had been attentive and willing to learn from Mr. Heinz while some of my other friends were out getting Italian ice, playing with makeup, and chatting on the phone. I also had no history of following heavy metal and rock band groups.

The following day was Saturday, and my family and I enjoyed the company of Grandma Pacita who was my mom's mother who flew in from the tropical island of Puerto Rico. Grandma was an excellent cook and so the kitchen soon was full of amazing aromas of jasmine rice, stewed beef with veggies, and fried plantains. Yum!

Before I knew it, the weekend was over and it was Monday. It's time to head back to school. I had a pep in my step and an unusual confidence within as if God was about to show up in my life again. I stayed quiet on the bus ride to school and prayed. *Lord, whatever happens, I trust you,* was my prayer.

The big yellow bus pulls into the school yard and I stay pretty cool, trusting that if God is real, He'll hear my prayer and respond accordingly. I make my way to my classroom after Bible devotions. The school had a practice of collecting all students into an auditorium first thing each morning to praise God, pray to God, and read a portion of the Bible before starting class, which was called Bible devotions.

As soon as I enter the door of my classroom, Mrs. Mazzy, the classroom monitor, greets me at the door. "Good morning Belle. You have a message to deliver to the school," expressed Mrs. Mazzy. Mrs. Mazzy continues by explaining, "God woke me up Friday night at eleven. to confirm to me that you have a warning to share with the school. You must share that warning without delay because lives depend on it. I have already cleared it with Principal Cunningham and we are directing grades fifth through twelfth to stay in the auditorium so you can be handed a microphone and you can deliver the message."

Wow! Did God show up in my life once again? With boldness, although I had never spoken to a large group of people before, I made my way back to the auditorium and grabbed the microphone. The words came pouring out of me and the tears as well. I shared my experience of seeing God and Satan fighting over my soul and witnessing God snatching my soul from Satan's grasp after beating Satan senseless. I expressed the dangers of certain rock and heavy metal music and exposed how Satan uses hidden messages in some music to manipulate our minds and hearts into steering away from

God. I then delivered the main warning. "God wants you to know that He created music for His people to praise and worship Him and only Him, not to worship any other," I proclaimed.

Then things got very serious. I saw the faces of many classmates, children, and teens from ages ten through eighteen. They were at a very impressionable age. Satan knows this. Satan knows if he gets a hold of our thoughtlife, and hearts at a young, impressionable age, He can cause us to be lost in the world, without God, without God's favor, and without God's protection. This is Satan's way of steering us down a path of destruction which will eventually lead to our death without God. Once God is out of the equation and we die, Satan then steals our souls and we then meet our destiny in the lake of fire referred to as hell.

"I cry out to you because I don't know exactly which ones of you listen to this rock and heavy metal in your free time at home, but please heed to the warning. Stop listening to this music. It may cost you your life!" I explained to the school. Fear rose among the crowd and it was silent. My heart cried out to them because I now understood how real hell is and the pain, agony, and hot fiery furnace that awaited my fellow classmates if they did not obey God's warning.

As I ended the message, I felt peace that I had complied and did what God requested of me. I also heard a clear, distinct voice in my spirit that said, "Well done." A public school setting would probably not have allowed my warning to be spoken out among the school nor would they have invited God to show up. Being a student at a God-seeking private school which provided Bible devotions every morning allowed me to experience God and welcome Him to show up in my life. I learned through this experience that God is always at work, and if we choose to have a relationship with Him and accept His invitation to be a part of what He is currently doing, we will hear Him speak. After hearing Him speak to us, we will have a crisis of belief and ask God to confirm what He wants us to do. Once He confirms, we can adjust, go forward in boldness, and obey and experience God for ourselves! Didn't God confirm what He had said to me in the bathroom through Mrs. Mazzy at the very same hour of the night? It was late, approximately 11:00 p.m., Friday, after my meeting with the teens in Mr. Heinz's class that God woke up Mrs. Mazzy while I was kneeling at the tub in my bathroom.

It was then that I began to realize that God is always working around us. He is working in our communities, in our churches, in our schools, in our homes, and in our cities. It is up to us to join Him in what He is doing. As soon as we realize what He is doing where we are, our lives and activities will be thrown into contrast to God and His activity. We cannot stay the way we are and go with God.

God pursues a continuing love relationship with you that is personal. God invites you to become involved with Him and a part of His work. God speaks by way of the Holy Spirit, through the Bible, prayer, circumstances, and the church. He reveals Himself, His purposes, and His ways through these channels.

God showing up in the bathroom was an invitation for me to work with Him and led me to a crisis of belief. Was I day dreaming or was this real? I asked God to confirm and I prayed on the school bus, putting my faith into action, telling God I trust in Him. A crisis of belief requires faith and action. Making the adjustment to put faith into action and prepare for God to show up in my life allowed me to then come to know God on a personal basis by experience as I obeyed Him and accomplished His work.

Sadly, a few years after my warning about heavy metal music to the school, two of my classmates had died very tragic deaths. Danny was accidentally killed in army training boot camp by inhaling too much of an expired tear gas bottle while confined in a small space. While exposure to tear gas does not commonly lead to death, expired tear gas can be very toxic. Susan had gotten into a relationship with an older man after high school graduation. Susan's boyfriend became obsessed and controlling with her and during an argument, he became physically abusive, grabbed a large kitchen knife, and stabbed Susan to death. He then chopped her body in several pieces. As painful as it is for me to admit this truth, both Danny and Susan were heavy metal followers.

CHAPTER 2

Joy and Peace

A FEW YEARS GO BY, and now I'm in love, engaged to be married, and pregnant! It's summer of 1988, and I'm in full baby mode, picking out baby names, and shopping for a crib, dresser, and rocking chair. It is a happy time for my parents and I as we prepare for the first grandchild to be born. Mom is sewing curtains, Dad is setting up the diaper changing table, and little brother, Adam, is placing toys in the toy chest already.

One summer day while attending church service, Brother Mario starts up a conversation with me. Mario was a mature man with an English accent, very friendly, well dressed, and polite. He asked me how my pregnancy was going and how the baby room preparations were coming along. I filled him in. Then Mario begins to share a vision God revealed to him, concerning myself and my unborn child.

Brother Mario shares that God showed him that I would be having a baby girl at 8 lbs and 4 oz and that she would be born on August 19 in a blue hospital room. Mario continues his vision and says, "God wants you to name your baby girl Joy Peace, and if you obey, you, Belle, will have joy and peace all the days of your life." Mario expresses that he saw me wearing a uniform in my career and traveling back and forth in between two islands. I found all this very interesting.

The time came for my baby girl to be born. And…you guessed it. She was born on August 19, 1988 weighing 8 lbs and 4 oz in a blue hospital room. Would I obey God and name her Joy Peace? Well, the funny thing about the name Peace is that grandma Pacita was named Paz. Pacita became her nickname over the years. Paz is the Spanish word for peace. So, naming my daughter after grandma was a win–win situation. Grandma fell in love with her first great grandchild, and I obeyed God.

The weather began to change a little during that August week in Long Island, New York. The weather was beginning to cool off a bit as summer was coming to an end. I developed a fever after giving birth so my hospital stay was extended to a five-day stay. While recovering, I not only began to bond with Joy, but also became a little withdrawn from my fiancé. The weather was not the only thing changing.

The truth is that although I loved Anthony, I didn't feel that we had what it took to last long term. I found myself praying about this situation during my hospital stay. Do I take a chance and marry him with doubts or do I just call off the wedding? A child was now in my arms and would be the glue that bonds Anthony and I for life either way.

After bathing Joy, I went to bed early one night at the hospital and had a dream. In my dream, I see Anthony on a line with millions of other people on this same long line. Anthony has shackles on his wrists, ankles, and neck. He seems to be in anguish, very agitated, miserable, and angry. I asked him what this long line was about, but he did not hear me. As I move to take a closer look at what was ahead, I see a bright light like from a huge fiery lake, and I then realize Anthony is in hell.

God reveals a spirit of lust upon Anthony's life and shows me that Anthony's father introduced him to that spirit of lust through magazines. As I look toward the front of this line, I see Anthony's dad, shackled, awaiting his turn to be thrown into the lake of fire.

When I awoke, I was gasping for air. I was trembling with fear and in shock of what I saw and learned. I calmed myself after catching my breath and prayed some more. *God, show me how to get out of this relationship if Anthony is not the man you have for me*, I prayed.

A few months later, we were approaching the holidays. I was prepping the house for guests and doing some major cleaning throughout. As I dug out storage containers from underneath the bed, I came across a stack of pornographic magazines, some of which dated back to the 1960s and 1970s. I knew some of these mags had been given to Anthony by his father considering that the dates and the legal age to purchase pornographic material is eighteen.

I kept my findings to myself and continued cleaning, praying, and trusting in God. The holidays went smoothly and Joy was now sleeping more which allowed me to sleep a little more. I did my best to meet Anthony's needs and keep him happy. Our happiness was short lived. One day, I found evidence of infidelities—earrings left by the bed and lipstick on his shirts.

As I reflected back on our relationship over the next few days, I came to the conclusion that Anthony and I did not in fact have what it took to make things last long term. His infidelities and magazines were signs of lust, not love. So I packed mine and Joy's things and left him.

A couple of years later, Joy was old enough to attend a head-start nursery. I encountered a problem while trying to enroll Joy in nursery school. Since Anthony and I never married, I needed to show proof of custody in order to get Joy in school. Anthony and I discussed this circumstance. We got into a heated argument. Whether out of bitterness, vengeance, or just pride, Anthony did not want to sign over custody to me.

We hired lawyers and went to family court. Prayer is key and my first line of defense in any circumstance. My parents and I prayed. I remembered what Brother Mario had told me in his vision. If I obeyed God in naming my child Joy Peace, I would have joy and peace all the days of my life. Could it be that what God was really referring to was that I would actually have my child (Joy Peace) and not lose custody of her?

I never entered a courtroom because Anthony's lawyer never showed up. We settled the case in the court house lobby with my lawyer calling the shots and Anthony agreeing to all the terms my attorney presented to him. Joy Peace was now legally mine! Obedience to God pays off!

As Joy grows up, she becomes an A honor roll student throughout high school and college. She speaks English, Spanish, and Italian and is my greatest accomplishment in life. She has formed a tight bond with her dad regardless of the past and she is my greatest delight.

God is a god of His word. When you obey Him, He happily rewards you beyond your expectations. God is eagerly waiting to bless His children who obey. Imagine the consequences if I had not obeyed. God knows the future before it happens and knows why He requests certain things of us. It is up to us to trust Him and put our faith into action. I have learned to obey God and leave the consequences up to Him.

CHAPTER 3

Jerry

IN THE SUMMER OF 1995, I begin working at a restaurant owned by a friend. I worked the morning shift as an opening manager, prepping food and managing the day crew. I had a few bright, young people working under me and enjoyed their youthful, carefree attitudes. There was one young man, however, that stood out of the crowd.

His name was Benny. He was very gothic, wearing black clothes almost every day, had skeletons on his jewelry, with long hair, and a serious, somewhat dark disposition. Benny was quiet, maybe too quiet. He did his job fairly well and rarely called in sick so that was sufficient for me.

Another one of my employees was named Jerry. Jerry was sweet, always cheerful, always reliable, and willing to go the extra mile at work. His face glowed and Jerry made my workload lighter. I didn't have to double check his work. It was always excellent. Getting to know Jerry over the year that I worked with him allowed me to learn that he was also an excellent student in high school, a mama's boy, and adored by his Christian family.

Prom night came along for the class of '95 in North Babylon, New York, and both Benny and Jerry planned their evening together. The night of the prom was a Friday night in May and both boys pulled into the parking lot of the restaurant to get their pay checks. I still remember the proud feeling I felt in my heart as they came out of the limousine they rented. They both came in with smiles, kissed me on the cheek, and put out their hands. I gladly handed them their paychecks, and they were off.

As Jerry took his check out of my hand, I heard a voice tell me, "This is the last time you'll see him alive." I knew instantly that this was the audible voice of God for I had heard His voice before. I ran after Jerry out into the parking lot. I caught Jerry just as he was about to enter the back of the long, black limousine. "Jerry! Jerry! Be careful tonight. I fear for your life! Be careful where you go tonight and who you go with." I warned. Jerry hugged me and assured me he would be careful. So I waved goodbye to both boys and the limo pulled off.

I held my breath as I walked back into the restaurant, shaking my head. I was perplexed. I was not happy. I distinctly heard God tell me that this would be the last time I would see Jerry alive as if there was nothing that was going to change Jerry's fate.

The very next morning was my day off as I only worked Monday through Friday. I sat in the living room and put on the television. The Long Island news came on. I froze. The news broadcaster mentions Jerry Contessa's name. It turns out that Jerry and Benny and their prom dates had driven to an after party and a night club out east on Long Island. A fight broke out among the crowd of people dancing on the dance floor. Someone pulled out a knife and Jerry got stabbed several times in the abdomen and chest. Jerry bled to death in Benny's car.

I can't say that I was surprised this time around. Jerry had been hanging out with Benny, and Benny was a dark soul. I had always sensed a dark presence with Benny. You see, when a person becomes open to receiving the Holy Spirit in their lives and accepting God as their Lord and Savior, things begin to happen. The Holy Spirit was obviously making me very sensitive to the spirit of death for some reason.

The question was why? To make me aware of the spirits around me, to make others aware of the spirits around them, to be warned and to forewarn others around me of the enemy that comes to steal, kill, and destroy so that I may come to know God on a more personal level and be a part of what God is doing around me and my home, community, church, and city. I met a god that was able to tell me life before it happened. Have you met this god?

While I was not able to save Jerry's life, Jerry did come from a very supportive Christian family. Jerry's family had made it very clear to me upon meeting them at the funeral that Jerry had already committed his life to Christ by accepting God as His Lord and Savior, which means Jerry had salvation and will be in heaven the day I hopefully arrive there. While Jerry's life was cut short, it's not forgotten. I will never forget him.

Shortly after Jerry's death, I resigned from the restaurant and moved onto a higher-paying position elsewhere. I continue to pray for Benny's dark soul to this very day. Word has gotten back to me throughout the years from former coworkers that Benny had a step sister and other friends that died. Certain family members had discontinued their relationship with Benny because of suspicions that Benny had been worshiping Satan in secret quarters and played a hand in certain people's deaths. I remain neutral, knowing Satan is the enemy who manipulates others that are not bound to God. My advice is to bind yourself to God and start every day with God, pray all throughout your day, and end your day with God. Whatever troubles are on your mind at the end of the day and unfinished business, stuff you could not finish during the day, leave them on God's shoulders. He can handle it for you. Rely on Him.

What a great and mighty God we have access to.

CHAPTER 4

Carol

MY BEST FRIEND, NAMED CAROL, lived in Greenlawn, Long Island, New York. Carol owned a house cleaning business. She was the woman that threw me my baby shower when I was pregnant with Joy. She was a blonde, blue-eyed, larger-than-life woman from Virginia. She was a member of Upper Room Church and choir as well. My brother and I were friends with Carol's daughter, Lilly, from school.

It was during the summer of 1997 when Carol's only child, Lilly, was killed in a car accident on the LIE, which is the Long Island Expressway. Lilly had plans to drive out to an amusement park with friends the next day. After work on a late Friday night, Lilly began her journey out east to her friend's home to enjoy a slumber party and then hit the road to the amusement park with friends early Saturday morning. She never made it to her friend's home. A man driving a van that night fell asleep behind the wheel. Since Lilly was driving a convertible with the top roof down, the initial impact was so hard that Lilly was thrusted out of the car and thrown to the ground. That's not what killed her. The van then hit her swinging around in a 360 degree circle, running over her body which was on the ground. That running over is what killed her.

My friend, Lilly, had a closed casket. Her body and face were too distorted to be shown to the public. My friend, Carol, was hurt, broken, heartbroken, but still standing. What was about to happen next in my journey with Carol would blow my mind forever. There are some things that happen in life that just leave you with absolutely no doubt at all that there is a God. How can I talk about God in the midst of such a tragedy? God is always at work and Satan is also always at work as well. To stay in tuned with God is the wise thing for all mankind to do. Let's see how God works.

After a year or so of Carol mourning, I decided it was time to return back to work with her. She needed time to mourn her only child and I understood that as a mom of an only daughter myself. I empathized with her and understood her need to reflect, be still in the presence of God, and make peace with all that had happened. God is in control. Carol knew this better than I.

I walked into her home which had a different dynamic. It was no longer Mom, Dad, and Daughter with the two dogs and a parakeet. There was one less in the home now. I expected to see a woman in distraught, sad, unraveled, and in despair. To my surprise, it was the "Thus saith the Lord," that came out of her mouth. For those of you reading this that don't know what that means, allow me to explain. "Thus saith the Lord" is God speaking from heaven through a human being on earth. When a person has been filled with the Holy Spirit, constantly seeking time with Him, continuously praying to Him, speaking to Him, keeping His commandments, and desiring to fulfill His will, God will speak through them. But God can and will speak through anyone and anything at any time He chooses to do so for He is God.

It was more than obvious that instead of pouting, being angry, and in despair, Carol had been seeking God in the midst of her great loss. I was stunned to be walking into the door and hearing God speaking through Carol. She clearly affirmed that I would be witness to much more in Carol's life and that this was not by accident. I began to brace myself knowing how God had revealed Himself to me in the past and expecting God to reveal more of Himself. I knew that it would be more than amazing.

I began to assist Carol in cleaning out her daughter's bedroom. I purchased the bedroom furniture to give Carol some comfort that the memory of Lilly would live on with me. I just felt that in the moment Carol needed to hear that from me. Carol smiled as if to thank me for the kind words. I could not replace her daughter nor her loss, but God knows that if I could, I would. I tried my best to be the best friend possible.

One day after cleaning houses, Carol and I came home to her Greenlawn house to take a break. When we walked into the house, we realize the dog is not barking or jumping for joy. Carol had two yellow Labradors that were both so friendly and smart. The dogs were obviously missing Lilly's presence. They knew she was gone. As Carol and I walk out to the backyard where the dog house is, we see vomit and blood on the ground. The dog was sick. A few days later, that yellow lab died. A few months later, the other Labrador had to be put down. Two months later, Carol's parakeet keeled over. There was nothing but feathers and a lifeless bird in the cage.

The following month, Carol's father in law became sick with cancer. Not too long after, Carol's good friend, Anna, was stricken with brain cancer. The most shocking of all was when Jimmy, Carol's husband who was a servant and a TV camera man at the church, plus an electrician by trade and a photographer by hobby, died.

It was one of the strangest experiences I can recall. Jimmy was the most humble, meek, honest, and faithful men that was full of the word of God and so happy all the time. It turned out that this foreman, skilled at his electrician job for over twenty-five years, electrocuted himself on the job on what would have been Lilly's twenty-third birthday. Two years after Lilly's death, her father Jimmy died on her birth date. Crazy! It was obvious that Jimmy's mind was not on his work but rather on his child that he missed tremendously.

Carol was now faced with burying her husband. It was apparent that death was all around us! Was I afraid? Sure. But if God is with me, who can stand against me? No one. Carol then hired me to help her clean out Jimmy's belongings after six months and sell his expensive camera equipment. I remember Jimmy using those cameras for weddings, anniversaries, and sweet sixteen photos for members of the church, neighborhood, and community. At the ripe age of fifty, he was gone.

After Carol mourned her husband, things got wild. Wilder than before, Belle? You ask. Yes, wilder than before! Carol and I set out to clean some houses together in the Huntington area of Long Island, New York. One autumn day, as we entered a burger joint to have lunch, we encountered danger. It is amazing how Satan is threatened by God's people. Allow me to explain.

Carol and I are standing on line in the fast food restaurant, deciding if we want burgers or fish sandwiches. In walks a man into the front door that looks homeless, not well dressed, somewhat of an alcoholic, appearing shabby, and not well groomed. The homeless-looking stranger walks straight up to us. He begins asking, "Who is Jim and Lilly Marie? The same way I killed both of them, I will kill you also!" And he walked out the door. Carol and I began to pray immediately, knowing a demonic spirit was just in our presence. We picked up our fish platters and headed to a table, continuing our prayers. I was in shock to see how much of a threat Carol was to Satan himself that he felt the need to threaten Carol's life in public.

I knew I was dealing with a spirit-filled, God-fearing, 100% sold-out-for-Christ woman when it came to Carol. But wow, I did not know to this level. When Satan feels so threatened, that he has to show up on your lunch break and threaten your very life, you are a real Christian, walking side by side with God and truly a threat to hell! I had never seen anything like it! How awesome is that? To think that Carol's very existence threatened Satan and hell to the point of Satan showing up in a burger joint! Do you get the full importance of this woman on earth? Do you get the full importance of you and your family and friends on this earth?

During our lunch break, as we began to chow down on our fish and chips, Carol says to me that she will write a book. I immediately recognized that she herself would NOT write the book but that the Holy Spirit, through me (Belle), would write the book. Carol was speaking through the Holy Spirit at the time that she was saying this. The Holy Spirit was claiming that a book would be written containing the details of Carol's life and death. Who better than I to write that book when I had a front row seat to every detail of her life and death.

The time came when Carol began to list her home for sale. Why not? Her family was now gone. Her daughter, her husband, the dogs, the parakeet, and her father in law all passed on. She had become a millionaire due to the insurance claim on her daughter's death and the life insurance on her husband's death, plus the selling of both homes. She had the home in Greenlawn and also a vacation home in Poconos, Pennsylvania. What a way to become a millionaire. It cost her everything!

In her loneliness, I tried to fill the void at least as a close friend. I tried to encourage her and just be there for her. But it was she that was there for me. One day, I went over to Carol's home just to hang out with my girlfriend. We went to the backyard and ate food and swung on the swing just like real girlfriends do. This was about to become my very favorite moment of Carol's life on earth. She and I sat there swinging like young girls on a summer day. All of a sudden, my girlfriend became another person!

I kid you not! Carol became someone else. That is an understatement! All of a sudden, her voice changed, her speech changed, her vocabulary changed. I became aware immediately that God took over Carol's body and was speaking directly to me. Do you even understand how awesome it is for the Creator of heavens, the universe, and earth and mankind to sit beside me on a swing and speak directly to me? I froze. It was the wildest day of my life!

God began to explain directly to me that He had walked into church at the Upper Room as the congregation was praising Him! There were times during Sunday gatherings at the local church that God, Himself, had descended down from heaven and, in spirit, walked into that church and sat down in the front row and no one had noticed. God, through Carol, began sharing with me that He wanted to do much more than what was already being done at the Upper Room church, but no one was paying attention. He was after the hearts of those that were sold out for Christ, not just going through the motions of being a Christian.

God explained that He longed to use those that were totally faithful to Him to save the souls of multitudes of unsaved people. The problem was that *the faithful* were not listening. God's heart was breaking before my very eyes. God, through Carol's body, was hanging out with *me* on a swing and His heart was breaking. *How do I comfort the heart of the King of kings and Lord of lords?* I asked myself.

Carol's face looked at me and said, "Share your story with others, Belinda. Tell them. Warn them that I exist. I am real. I know all. I see all. I created each and every one of them and I desire to bless them both on earth and in heaven. They simply need to accept, follow, and obey my commandments and deny themselves."

Allow me to explain what this means. Accepting God is simply to accept that His son, Jesus Christ, died on the cross for our sins simply because He was the only royal blood line to God the Father that was sinless and holy and could die in our place to reconcile us back to the Father in our fallen, sinful nature. Our flesh is weak. Our own will, our own perception of things, and our own desires are weak, whereas God's guidance is strong for He knows all things, sees all things, and hears all things.

So let's say that we have an opportunity to take advantage of another person for our own gain. God sees our intent. Love is about giving, not taking. Whatever we take with the wrong intent or steal, we will lose three times the amount somewhere down the line in our future. Love is all about giving. God gave His only begotten son to die on the cross for our sins. God made the ultimate sacrifice for mankind. Would you put your only son on a cross to die for others? I thought not.

After a good fifteen minutes of conversing with the master of the universe, Carol came back to me, in her own voice, speech, and tone. She was not even aware of what had just taken place. It was a glimpse into God's heart and the experience was clearly just for me. It is my truth, my very own one-on-one reality that God loves us and is concerned about the salvation and destiny of every single one of us. We are the reason His heart beats, the very center of His attention, and a relationship with us is His desire.

In the snap of a finger, things were back to normal and Carol asked if I would like some iced tea to drink. I had just been in the presence of royalty and had been frozen in time, unable to move just like the time I saw God in my yellow bathroom. A hard drink was my honest desire but iced tea was sufficient. But then, Carol explained she had some bad news for me and I became anxious for that hard drink.

Carol had been experiencing some unusual, sharp pain and went to the doctor for some testing. Soon after, the doctor discovered terminal cancer in her bones. My friend was dying. She introduced me to the medication she would soon be taking—morphine. I stayed strong in the moment, but I was crying a river inside. She and I had been surrounded by death, but now death was coming for her.

I hugged my friend and still stayed strong. She had been so strong for so long that she set an excellent example for me. Breaking down in front of her was not an option. She and I together had gotten through the deaths of Jimmy, Lilly, the two dogs, the parakeet, and her father in law and the threat of a homeless-looking man in the burger joint. Were we going to allow this to fill us with depression or would we continue the good fight? To continue the good fight was the only route!

Carol and I put her Greenlawn home up for sale. It was sold to a retired pastor. Then, we packed up all her belongings and shipped them to Texas. Carol had befriended a man that was an evangelist in the Texas area and she felt God leading her to leave a certain amount of her insurance winnings to this evangelist for God's word to be shared on television. Her desire was to fund and see the beginning of this television ministry take off.

The day came for Carol to hop on the plane to set off on her Texas destination. Before she left New York, she and I had one more meal together. We shared memories together, laughter, and recalled good moments at work. She thanked me for being a faithful employee and friend. She explained that there would be times when I would go through hard times and God's hand of protection would be over my life simply because I had been a faithful friend to her. I found out years later that it would be just so as Carol had said.

As she and I exited the diner that evening, hugging and saying our goodbyes, I heard God's audible voice again. "This will be the last time you see her alive. The next time you see her, she will be lying in a coffin." I knew it would be so for I already knew the voice of God. Then, she drove off in her Nissan Maxima and I was left with my tears in the parking lot. My heart broke that night for I knew I would never hear her voice again, look into her blue, sparkling eyes again, hear her sing, and laugh with her like girlfriends do. God was preparing me for the end of my buddy's life.

I sat in my car reviewing Carol's life in my mind. I thought of the very first time I met her, Jimmy, and Lilly at the Upper Room church in Dix Hills, New York. I recalled the many times she took me under her wing to counsel, teach, guide, nurture, or just hang out with me. I revisited her many losses in life and the fact that her faith was not shaken. It was as if she grew much stronger spiritually and closer to God. Carol taught me the bar of excellence in the work field and that working as if God is your boss can never bring bad results.

My tears started to flow. I began to realize that she had purposely deposited the very best of herself in me before leaving me. What a huge investment she had made in me. I realized how blessed I was in the moment and began to lift my hands and praise my God. My God who supplied all, has given me all, has ordained my every footstep, put His only son on a cross for me, and poured excellence and favor in me. What a great and mighty God He is all the time.

I can't reiterate enough how great this God is because of the things I've seen. I know it may sound insane to some of you, but I assure you as confident as I am in the Practical Nursing degree I gained in Puerto Rico and the bachelor's degree I obtained in Social Work at Molly College on Long Island, I have also attended the university of experiencing God Himself in my everyday life and I am sane.

The day came where I received the bad news. I was working my weekend job at a hardware store in Deer Park, New York, when Mom walked in. It was very rare, almost never, that Mom showed up at my place of employment so I suspected something was up. She approached me saying that Carol had died. I broke down. I even yelled! I quickly ran to the back break room so that I could have a moment with just Mom. I knew it was coming, but losing Carol was such a big loss that even God preparing me didn't fully cushion the blow.

I had worked so hard to keep her alive, administering the morphine when she needed it, comforting her, supporting her, praying for her, feeding her the proper foods, and keeping sugar out of her system. I needed her to live longer. I needed her to continue. I needed to see God's hand move in her life one more time. But God is the author and Creator of mankind. He gives life and He takes it away. He is all powerful and the highest authority and government that exists. He takes those He wants when He wants.

Mom, Dad, my daughter Joy, and I, including Brother Adam, all went to the funeral. So it was, as God had told me, that the next time I saw Carol, she was lying in a coffin. As I approached her coffin in the viewing of her body, I wasn't sad. I was rather joyful. As I looked at her face one last time, I told her, "I'll see you later, my buddy." Meaning, I vow that no matter what happens in life, I will never abandon my belief in my God! I will do whatever it takes to be sold out for Christ and be in constant communion with my God and make it to heaven.

The story of Carol does not end there. The evangelist who had been given millions of dollars by Carol was at the funeral home. As I approached to greet him, I felt a strong presence of God around him. His name is Clement and he's from Australia. He has been able to foretell the future many times in the past. If you've seen him on television, it's thanks to my friend, Carol, for sure. I shook Clement's hand and felt as though God himself was piercing His eyes right through me. I became transparent in the moment. My knees began to tremble.

I greeted Clement, letting him know that I was Carol's best friend. He knew right away that I was Belle for Carol had mentioned me to him before she had died. Then, Carol's sister approached me. She had a similar face to Carol but with dark hair. She begins by saying hello to me. She then begins expressing how the last days of Carol's life and death played out. I braced myself knowing that something heavy was about to be laid on me, if you know what I mean.

Carol's sister, Lynne, began to express how Carol wanted me to know that I should continue to be successful in God and move forward even though she is gone. Then, Lynne expressed to me that during Carol's last days of life, she had cancer sores all over her entire body, mouth, tongue, lips, and esophagus. Carol had whispered to Lynne that an angel had presented himself to her. The angel asked her, "Carol, do you want to go home today or tomorrow?"

Carol whispered in her cancer-filled throat, "Tomorrow, for I am still praying for those that I am leaving behind on this earth."

Now, I, as a healthcare worker and a cancer survivor myself, can testify that cancer hurts! It is a very sharp pain that carries throughout the body that lets you know death can be very near. I, myself, had cancer of the uterus. The cancer came as a result of being extremely overweight. When a female body is very overweight, many things can go wrong. My gynecologist of twelve years had been warning me against gaining more weight. He proclaimed that gaining more weight and becoming obese was a danger for cancer.

I slowly, throughout the years, began gaining more and more weight as a result of eating fast foods and not exercising on a daily basis. As I switched careers and then began to work on a heart-monitored floor in a hospital in West Islip, New York, I then became very obese as a result of both the stress of the job itself and the compensations of the patients that had improved during their hospital stay. Some recent patients would come back to the hospital to visit and give their thanks with high-calorie food in their hands. I found myself weighing 254 lbs during December of 2011.

I freaked out seeing the digital numbers on the scale. Being 254 lbs on a hospital scale was a definite eye opener for me.

Getting back to cancer… I had begun bleeding in a perfuse state. The excessive bleeding was a clear sign that something was very wrong. As I went to the doctors to inquire what was going on, Carol and her cancer problems came to mind. How did she stay so strong for so long? Doctors found me to have cancer, which required a hysterectomy to be done. Both the cancer itself and the surgery were extremely painful. But I am alive and well today to tell my story.

I can testify that cancer hurts! Carol's throat, tongue, mouth, skin, and stomach were full of cancer sores and painful blisters. The bone cancer had spread all throughout her body and fully consumed her. I imagine if it was me, I would have told the angel, "I want to go to heaven right now, this very second!" For Carol to be in excruciating, viscous pain all over her entire body, yet still be concerned about others was amazing to me. Carol was a trooper until her very last breath.

The angel said, "Okay." Carol lived for another twenty-four hours. She mumbled under her breath, and spoke in tongues, a heavenly language, as she prayed during those last hours of her life. I had never in my life heard of such selflessness other than Christ Himself dying on the cross for you and I. What bravery, what faith, and what love she had in her heart to deal with so much pain yet be so filled with the Holy Ghost, God's love, and God's will. My God! Carol was a true example of how to walk in God's love.

Whether we believe in God or not, we will go through turmoil, trials, and tribulations. Hard times will come. I have learned through Carol that having access to God allows me to have peace, mercy, and favor from God and assurance that He's got me! No one ever said that following God was going to be roses, but if they persecuted Christ and Christ was sinless, I knew better than to think life as a Christian would be a walk in the park. For I am not sinless!

I miss my friend. I miss everything about her. I value the time I had with her for it is priceless. Love gives. Carol gave. I'm giving back by telling her story. Who better than I to tell it when I had a front row seat to her life? I'm honored to have befriended, been taught, and loved by her. Carol was a woman that taught by being a living, breathing example of God's love, 24/7, even on her death bed.

CHAPTER 5

Mom

MY MOM, MARIA, WAS THE oldest of seven daughters and the third oldest of nine children. Mom had two older brothers. She was raised in Bronx, New York. Maria was raised as a Pentecostal by my grandma. She married Dad at twenty and I'm very proud to say she was married to Dad for forty-nine years. Maria was sweet, hard-working, a God-fearing woman, honest, and, most of all, a woman that knew how to love others unconditionally. There are few people that can love others the way Mom did.

Mom was the strongest woman I knew, besides Grandma and Carol. I myself had no choice but to become strong after the example that these three women had set before me. I remember Mom being a prayer worrier. When Mom prayed, it was like, watch out! Things happened when Mom prayed. It was as if she had a direct line to heaven. God listened to her and acted swiftly. What kind of woman stirs the heart and hand of almighty God in such a way? Ah, that is the major question.

Obedience moves the hand of God. Obedience to His word or the Bible and obeying His commandments stirs His heart and hand. Seeking God and His will instead of our own wills touches His heart. It's as if He seeks out those that obey Him and responds to their prayers, petitions, and desires. When we seek to please Him and we put Him first, He then puts us first. It is really that simple.

I recall the day I was on my way to work at age twenty. It was Fall and I was in route to the bank I was employed at when Mom called out my name. I turned around and walked back to her. She explained to me that I was in disobedience toward God and as a result would be out of a job by Friday. Wow! What strong words to hear from my mom on a Thursday. The very next day, I was escorted out the door of the bank by security.

What I did to lose my job was I breached client confidentiality. I looked up the address and telephone number of the female that my boyfriend was cheating on me with. I exchanged words with her and told her a thing or two. So not worth losing my job over. But there it is, the truth.

This is just one of many examples of how God used Mom in my life. Mom was a trooper! She was an undercover agent for God Himself at times. She spoke in tongues, the heavenly language, that I told you about. One day, I awoke early in the morning to her voice, speaking a heavenly language over me. Mom then began to interpret this heavenly language, telling me that I will obey God whole heartily in the future. She began to explain that I would not remain in my disobedience and rebellion toward God, but that I would rather surrender all to Him one day.

By my own admission, I have surrendered all to God. My desires, goals, fleshly desires, my daughter, and everything is surrendered to God daily. In other words, my life is not my own. Everything I have and everything that I am belongs to Him and is attributed to Him. I live for Him.

Is there any greater purpose in life than to serve the King of kings and the Lord of lords? If you had lived my life, from the time that I first heard God's audible voice at age fifteen under the leadership of Mr. Heinz, to then Carol, to then the days of now, where I am successful, accomplished, joyful, full of faith, and His favor, which way would you have gone? What route would you have taken? What route have you currently taken in your life?

Mom's greatest impression on my life was her loving others unconditionally. I will admit, this is a struggle at times. But it's getting easier. I am a giver not a taker. But I am stubborn and from New

York with a New York attitude. Those of you from New York know what I'm talking about. Some of the smartest, wisest, most productive people in the United States are located in New York. We are a people that just don't take nonsense from other people. We are not dreamers or talkers. We are doers. Anyone trying to blow smoke our way risks the chance of being trampled upon, to put it mildly. My attitude remains a work in progress.

Mom sewed both on a sewing machine and by hand. She made my curtains, bed spread, and canopy cover for my canopy bed. She learned how to make macramés (plant holders), hand-made dolls, clothing, and scarfs. Mom was multitalented in the kitchen, arts and crafts, and in her love for God. Aside from being a prayer warrior, speaking in tongues, and loving others unconditionally, Mom also gave of herself to others. She babysat children in the neighborhood, helped people financially, and gave advice to and befriended those that were difficult to get along with.

The love I received from Mom sometimes smothered me as I am her miracle child. Mom confronted difficulty getting pregnant. After seeing a specialist for over a year in Manhattan, I was finally created. It took Mom six years in total to get pregnant with me. I knew I was greatly loved by this woman my entire life. She showed me that constant love all day, every day, for forty-two years until she died.

When one is loved and adored on such a high level for so long, one knows that God exists for it is God who loves us through others. God has been so good to me for so long. Has He been good to you? Is there anyone that has loved and adored you so much that you just knew God truly existed? Yep, that's another example of God's love!

I retired in 2012 and flew down to the tropical island of Puerto Rico where I reside today. I have a vacation home in Puerto Rico right behind my parents' home and decided to stay in it for a while. In 2013, Mom became ill. She, I, and Dad went out for dinner at a local restaurant by the beach. Hey, tropical living is good. While Mom was chewing on her chicken, she began to choke. I had to do the Heimlich maneuver on her and, yes, it was scary.

Mom survived dinner and I remained calm on the outside but scared on the inside. The next day, Mom choked again. The question was, why would a woman who has been able to swallow her food with no issues for sixty-eight years now have issues swallowing her food two days in a row? In order to sustain life, we need to eat, breath, and eliminate. Mom began to have trouble breathing while lying down at night time. Two of the three things we need to sustain life were being interrupted. As a trained healthcare worker, I became very concerned.

Not only did my hospital experience kick in and tell me something was very wrong, but I also saw the spirit of death appear again. I knew Mom was living her last days. I called my brother, Adam, in Florida to warn him that Mom was dying. Adam told me I was just panicking because instead of this being one of my patients at the old hospital, this was Mom so it was personal. I assured Adam that this was not about panic, this was about God taking His daughter home.

God can take anyone He wants whenever He wants for He is God. It was hard for me to swallow the truth of God taking her but it's true that she had served her purpose. She nurtured Dad, served as a really good wife to Dad for forty-nine years, and my best friend for forty-two years. She had mentored, served, worked for, and prayed for many throughout her life. God obviously wanted His daughter home with Him now.

Mom was diagnosed with esophageal cancer and died in July of 2014. I totally value and cherish the days that I had with her. During her last days, she prayed for others that she was leaving behind. Very much like Carol, Mom was more concerned about the loved ones she was leaving behind rather than herself. These two women displayed selfless love, and I had a front row seat to this love. I have a lot to live up to.

It reminds me of the selfless love Christ displayed on the cross for you and I. It also reminds me of the very reason we call ourselves Christians for we are Christ-like. We are a blessed people to be able to receive Christ as our Lord and Savior and have access to eternal life through His son. Those of us that actually walk the Christian walk, not just talking the talk, know His love and His promises.

Allow me to break down one of God's promises. God promises eternal life to all those that believe in Him, confess Him as their Lord and Savior, and who keep His commandments. I don't know about you, but eternal life sounds awesome to me. If such a thing exists, don't you want access to it? You mean life exists beyond this earth? Yes. The answer is yes!

I took care of Mom for ten months before God took her home. It was amazing. She knew she was leaving this earth even before I did and even before being diagnosed. She was too much! I remember her walking out onto the patio area of the house and telling me face to face that she was preparing to leave this earth. That was in January of 2014. She knew. She began calling her lawyer to put all of her finances and affairs in order.

By the time Mom was properly diagnosed with cancer, it had already spread throughout 50 percent of her body. She was obviously sick for a long time and was not aware of it. This is why some refer to cancer as being a silent killer. There is yet another common thread between Mom and Carol and cancer that I want to expose to my readers.

Carol had breast cancer about fifteen years prior to her diagnoses with bone cancer. She had beat the breast cancer according to doctors after those doctors had removed a portion of Carol's breast. But as you can read, Carol then died of bone cancer which means her body did still in fact had cancer in it. Likewise, Mom had a portion of her right breast removed back in 1988. Yet Mom later on died of esophageal cancer in 2014. Mom's death was yet another example of doctors cutting out cancer years prior, but cancer still lived in her body.

What I would like to expose to my readers is that diet, exercise, lots of water, and much less sugar, calcium, and protein help to lower the risk of cancer. Just cutting out the cancer is not sufficient.

Mom's funeral was like no other. I had two pastors under the same roof. One pastor was from the east coast of Puerto Rico and the other was from the west coast of Puerto Rico. It was a combination of God's very best to say goodbye to another one of God's very best! *Death, where is thy sting?* was the gist of Mom's funeral. In other words, *Death, where is your victory?* For those who are faithful to God, God is also faithful to them.

Allow me to break that down as well. During Mom's last days on this earth, she was praying. She was praying for family, friends, and those who don't know God as their Lord and Savior. She was literally praying for some of you people she didn't even know. Mom didn't need to know you in order to love you. She loved you unconditionally anyhow.

She sat in her hospital bed on a Friday night telling me she loved me. I was exhausted by Sunday night. After Dad and I spent three days straight in the hospital, both Dad and I needed showers and sleep. On Sunday night, I recognized that Mom started going in and out of consciousness. Mom's blood pressure dropped very low. As an experienced health care worker, I knew what that meant. No more pain medicine by law.

I leaned over Mom and told her, "Mom, your blood pressure has dropped very low and they will not administer anymore pain medicine at this point. If you are going to leave this earth, do it very soon. You have enough pain medicine in your system to last you throughout Monday afternoon. You don't need this earthly body anymore. Allow the Holy Spirit to take you home." Then I prayed over Mom that God would have mercy upon Mom and take her quickly!

Dad and I kissed her and went home to rest. The rest was in God's hands. As I woke up Monday morning at 8:00 a.m., I heard God's audible voice telling me to go see that He is faithful to those that are faithful to Him. I knew at that moment God had heard my prayer, been merciful, and took Mom home. I knew she was no longer alive nor in pain.

I didn't want Mom to linger in pain, holding onto life for my sake or Dad's sake. I wanted her home with her Creator! God heard my cry, drew near to His faithful daughter, and grabbed her before her pain medicine ran out in her system. I woke up Dad. "Dad, get up! Let's run to the hospital and check on Mom. God told me that Mom's already dead in life but alive in spirit with Him."

Dad and I arrived at the hospital around 8:45 a.m. As we entered Mom's hospital room, Mom was breathless and her body was still very warm to the touch. My experienced nursing side knew Mom had expired around 8:00 a.m. when God had woken me up.

It's okay that Dad and I were not there until her last breath because she was already falling into an unconscious state and she would not have even known if we were there. Dad and I had left her in the best of hands—the hands of God—when we had prayed over her. But if I know Mom, she was still praying until completely unconscious. Praying for me and for all of you because that's what moms do and that's what an awesome woman of God does.

If you're reading this now, it's because Mom prayed for you and God heard her prayers on her death bed. People died for you to hear about God and the benefits of knowing Him. It's not just religion, it's not fanaticism, it's not just people looking for a cause, a following. It's all about a real God that loves you, died for you, and wants to have a real, daily relationship with you. He yearns to meet you daily, chat with you, be there for you, and show up in your life. Will you allow this God to befriend you and have your back like no one else can?

CHAPTER 6

Me

On a hot summer day in August of 1994, myself and a friend named Tony drove out to the flatlands in Queens, New York. The flatlands are an area where young people gather to do some illegal racing. NYPD, forgive me! Tony and I joined the crowd as we rooted the cars on, picked our favorites, and placed bets. People climbed the trees for a better view and females cheered in the crowd.

A motorcycle rider had spun his tires in the tar, prepping as he was next in line to race. The motorcycle rider did not realize that a white Ford Mustang was behind him. The heat from the hot August sun had softened the tar and the motorcycle had kicked up some of that tar onto the white Mustang. It was simply an accident, unintentional. The man from the white Mustang stepped out of the vehicle, exchanged words with the bike rider, and then quickly took off.

Tony and I just happened to witness this because it took place right in front of us. About twenty minutes went by, and, all of a sudden, I heard a voice tell me to move three feet to the right. So, I grabbed Tony by the arm and moved three feet to the right. Tony asked me, "What are we moving for?"

I answered, "Just do it." As we refocus our eyes on the races, a white van pulls up in front of me. The sliding door of the white van opens up. What happened next would shake me.

The man from the white Mustang was now standing in front of me in the white van holding a rifle! I froze. I then put my eyes downward. The rifleman then fired several shots. Those shots were so loud as they were aimed toward someone right next to me. Then, the rifleman took off. Since my eyes were facing the ground already, a dead body came into my view. It was the motorcycle rider, the one that had kicked up tar onto the Mustang! His lifeless body laid there before my eyes—one shot in the head, the second in the chest, and the third in his leg.

What manner of God is this that He would send me a warning through the Holy Ghost and save my life? He already put His only son on the cross as a sacrifice of royal blood for me, He already gave me a way of salvation and eternal life. Now, He's going to save and preserve my very life?

Tony asked me, "Belle, what made you move three feet over to the right just moments before the shooting took place?"

My response was simply, "I heard a familiar voice and I know the voice of my Master, so I obeyed!" Tony was in awe! He had not realized how close of a relationship I had with God until that day. Tony was beside himself. He realized we, not me, but we were alive because of God and His benefits of supplying the Holy Spirit to guide us with a warning. My God, our Creator, is awesome beyond your wildest dreams! He's simply a right-on-time God, an all-knowing God, a real God, a miracle God, a transforming God, an in-your-face, saving-my-butt, and right-in-the-nick-of-time God!

I dare you to prove me otherwise! I dare you! From music to the birth of my child, to my bf, to my career, to my teenage years, and to my present, my God is God and no one can prove differently. I challenge you to try God. You've tried alcohol. You've tried love. You've tried the world and all it has to offer. You've tried rebellion. Some of you have tried drugs. Some have tried becoming millionaires. Now, try God! He delivers for He is the master of the universe, the moon, and the stars; the ultimate, supreme, and only Creator of earth, man, and all living things.

On another hot summer night, that same summer, more happened. I was in a town called Wyandanch. I was exiting a beverage shop that my cousin owned with two big glass bottles of fruit juice in a brown bag in hand. As I exited the store, I found myself surrounded by a circle of girls. Now, we all know that females can be catty, especially females from New York. Wrapped around a total misunderstanding were six females surrounding me as I walked along the sidewalk of Straightpath Avenue in Wyandanch, New York. These six females began accusing me of something I was not in fact guilty of.

These girls were hunting blood. They were about to jump me. What crossed my mind as I stood there listening to the girls was *God help me*! As I prayed quickly, I also thought of breaking the glass bottles that I held in my hands, breaking them against the sidewalk and cutting my way out of the situation at hand! What happened you ask? Hahaha. What do you think happened?

I prayed silently and all of a sudden God showed up! He showed up in a way that blew my mind!

Dad had purchased a ten-speed bike for me at age fifteen. I had a love affair with my ten-speed bike as I peddled along the neighborhood of Phoenix Drive, Lakeway Drive, and Nevada Road in North Babylon, New York. I was a regular biker along the neighborhood of North Babylon and Wyandanch, New York as a teenager. Ahhh! Those were the good old days!

This guy, named Curtis, out of nowhere showed up! Curtis was three years older than me but lived on Lakeway Drive around the corner from me. Curtis didn't know me directly but knew my face from riding my bike around the way. All of a sudden, Curtis showed up! He broke through the circle of girls that threatened my life that night. Curtis came right up to me and escorted me out of the circle. His words were, "Belinda, I haven't seen you in so long. How are you? Allow me to carry your bags and walk you to your car." God is right on time all the time! Curtis, wherever you are, thank you!

I don't know about your current god but my God is a right-on-time God all the time!!! Now I don't want to suggest that I couldn't help myself out of the situation. But doing it my way, breaking glass bottles across the sidewalk to slash some faces, could have caused harm or death to someone and landed me in jail. I was praying and God showing up was my better and best defense, of course! That's all I'm saying here.

Around age twenty-one, I started dating a young man from Queens, New York, named Charles. He was a big motorcycle fan who owned a few bikes himself. From time to time, Charles would take me for motorcycle rides at very high speeds and, wow, I welcomed that wild, dangerous vibe. One day, after a nice bike ride along the ocean of the Long Island Sound, Charles decided to get high on some illicit drugs as we entered his apartment.

This quickly became a problem. His behavior toward me became irate as he was agitated at anything and everything I said and did that day. I became quiet and still thinking that would calm him. But no. He then became angry thinking that I was ignoring him. Before I knew it, Charles was pushing me up against the wall with a gun pressed against my cheek. Fear arose, sweat was running down my face, and Mom and God were all I could think about. Under my breath, I cried out to God, *Lord, my Master, how will you get me out of this one?* The doorbell rang!

It was just another day where God protected His child for His purpose. I was obviously being protected by God and preserved because Carol and others would later on have an impact on my life that I would then share with you. Yes, these are extraordinary and supernatural events. The average person that simply believes that God exists does not normally experience these things. Our God is not an ordinary God! He knew we human beings would mess up when He created us. The Bible states that God created us in His likeliness and image. What does this mean to you and I? He saw Himself in us and therefore made a way to save us by putting His own son on the cross as a sacrifice for us. There goes that unselfish, unconditional, agape love!

I'm imperfect, a sinner just like you yet I was willing to depend on Him, believe in Him, listen to His voice, take heed to His warnings, and pray, as a first line of defense, after accepting Him as my Lord and Savior and being water baptized. This works. My God has never let me down, never. I challenge you to try Him out in your life and see for yourself. He is hands down the most awesome God ever! I would have to write another book to even come close to telling you all that He has done for me. I can't wait to hug, kiss, and thank Him up close in the heavens some day!

I recall working at the hospital and being exposed to a serious virus that threatened my life. It was an overwhelming experience. I had multiple patients in the hospital that week that had all been exposed to a superbug. Superbugs are very resistant to certain antibiotics. Superbugs are viruses that can cause death if not detected and treated quickly and properly. It appears that when I handled some of the patients and their lab samples, I became contaminated myself.

After a rash broke out on my body with a very high fever, I knew I needed to take time off from work to treat myself, stay away from contaminating anyone else at the hospital, and heal. It was good nursing practice and awareness that saved me that time around. I thank God for the opportunity to have gained the skills and awareness I have. Would Satan have loved to snuff me out with that virus and keep me from sharing my truth? Sure. Not this time Satan! God is in control!

Let's go deeper. What do I have that separates me from others? Well, I have a girlfriend that I attended high school with named Anne. Anne was Italian and an excellent student. I remember hanging out with her as a teen after school hours. Her mom was an awesome cook, best baked ziti and stuffed raviolis you can imagine. Anne's mom was old school, always cooking, cleaning, watching over the kids, and catering to her husband.

While digesting my fresh marinara sauce meal that day, I laid back with Anne across the big sofa in the family room to listen to music. Anne and I both loved the music of Amy Grant as we began to sing *Al Shaddai*. It brings back such sweet memories of my youth. Ahhh, to be young again! Youth, don't throw your life away! Be productive, serve God, and you won't be disappointed for there is no greater cause to live for!

Anne began to question me about the message I had delivered to the school the day before. She had many questions concerning what I saw, heard, and felt in my spirit in the yellow bathroom that night. I answered all of her questions with excitement to share this wild experience! Anne sat upright on the sofa, looked at me, and said, "Belle, there is a price to pay for following and obeying God."

I became saddened right away realizing that Anne may not be willing to pay the price. So I questioned her. "Anne, are you telling me that you are not willing to pay the price to serve Him?" I asked.

Anne looked up at me and said, "It costs too much." My heart sank as I immediately felt fear for Anne. I knew her words and decision would cost her more than what she ever anticipated.

It would be twelve years later as Anne and I were approaching our late twenties that Anne's life would change dramatically. Anne was taking the *pill* referring to birth control. But Anne was also smoking cigarettes. What do you think happened? Anne suffered a stroke as a result of combining cigarette smoking with the *pill*. Anne still suffers from the side-effects of that stoke today, but her heart has now fallen into place with God's will. Anne understands that God had mercy on her life for she is still alive and now faithful no matter what the cost! Isn't that something?

I'm not at all suggesting that anyone that is not willing to follow God 100% will then suffer a stroke. I'm simply observing that God knows how to get His message across, hence why I'm here to reveal my life to you and save you the hardship of going down the wrong path without God. Why anyone would want to live without God guiding them through their life is beyond me.

When we purchase a new car, the car comes with a manual. That manual tells us how to get the upmost benefits and usage of that vehicle. We will never tap into the true potential of that new car if we don't read the manual and become familiar with all the features available at our fingertips. Likewise, we humans will not know our true purpose nor tap into our full potential in this life nor eternity if we are avoiding God, our Creator, and the Bible which is our manual.

Wake up! Wake up all of you backsliders! Awaken your spirits and fall in love with your first love once again! You know His voice. You know He loves you. Fall in love with Him once again. He'll take you back, no questions asked. For those of you who don't know what a backslider is, it's simply a person that used to know God, serve God, but then left God to do their own will instead of God's will.

Being a backslider has heavy consequences, such as seven times the original amount of evil spirits that originally attacked you when you were not familiar with God's ways to begin with.

Who on earth wants to become familiar with evil spirits as if life is not difficult enough as it is? I've had my share of sensing bad spirits around me and it never becomes easier. Each time an evil spirit arises, it's a stronger spirit than the last. I can recall a time when I worked at a restaurant/bar where I had multiple friends stop in to have a drink and visit me in a little town called Brentwood. Not all of my acquaintances were innocent.

A friend, named Lathan, stopped in one night and things went left very quickly. Lathan was a well-known drug user and seller in Brentwood. This particular evening, Lathan walked into the restaurant wired, under the influence of crack cocaine, and he started pushing the owner's buttons. Something came over me. I saw Bear, the bouncer, grab a rifle and I jumped into action. I never ran so fast in my life.

Before I knew it, I was standing between Bear and Lathan with a rifle in my face! I thought to myself, *I've been here before!* I prayed in my spirit, *Father, here we go again! Lathan is a lost soul but have mercy on him Father and spare our lives tonight,* I cried. I began to calm down the situation. I told Bear, "I'll put him in my car and take him home right now. He'll be out of your hair in a flash," I explained. Bear put the rifle down and Lathan ran to my vehicle. Problem solved.

Deescalating situations has become of a life-long responsibility for me both in my careers and personal life. Being part of the solution as opposed to being part of the problem is what we, as Christians, are supposed to be doing on a daily basis. Why would I stick my neck out and put myself in the line of fire for a drug addict? Because Lathan is God's child also. Jesus died on the cross for Lathan as well. It's that simple. Lathan now has a relationship with God, twenty-five years later. God is merciful!

I can go on and on revealing the many times that God spared my life! I was held at gun point when the restaurant I was employed at was being robbed. My initial thought was, *Okay, guns are becoming so familiar to me. I don't fear them any longer.* But then one of the robbers cocked his gun and fear became a reality once again. They just wanted the money. They got the money and took off in a black-stretched limousine. Talk about doing a crime in style!

I have been through some things just as you have. We all have a story. My story is God-filled, God-inspired, and God-ordained because I obey Him and His voice. My life has shown me that obedience to God pays off! Do you agree? I can't imagine my life without Him. I know His benefits. I know His voice. I know Him. I am honored to know His ways and be preserved by Him! I would love nothing but the same for all of you.

He is the ultimate experience one can have. Vodka, romance, marijuana, pills, money, jewelry, fame, and success has nothing on God! He is the supreme, ultimate experience! I've lived it up in the Hampton's, New York City, and all over the east coast of the United States. I've partied in mansions in Muttontown and Oyster Bay, Long Island. I've seen some of the best that the world has to offer and it's nothing compared to what God has to offer.

CHAPTER 7

Let's be Real

IT'S NOT NORMALLY COOL NOR popular to be a religious fanatic. I'm not interested in being a religious nut either. While this may be the sad truth, consequences come with that reality if we decide to never connect and follow our God. I simply chat with Him just like I'm chatting with you right now. The same way we chat with folks we barely know via social media and the internet. Have you chatted with God lately?

I recall wanting to work in a hospital setting to help others. I remember the desire being strong and constant. I remember God showing up and opening doors that seemed impossible to open. I knew it would be a challenge.

You see, at the time this desire for being in the nursing field arose in me, I was already twenty-two years old and living with Grandma in Puerto Rico. Although I am of Puerto Rican descent, I was born and raised in New York my whole life and knew nothing about the Spanish language that was ruling this island. I put myself in nursing school here in Puerto Rico and purchased a Spanish dictionary and a medical terminology dictionary.

Yes, not knowing the language, I passed my two-year course for my practical nursing degree and finished my practice. All things are possible for those who put God first. I've come to know that when I have a very deep desire for something good, it's God that puts that desire in me. Since He put the desire in me, He also provided all that I needed to succeed. Professors that were understanding to my language crisis, government funds and a scholarship to pay for my schooling, and a grandmother that provided a car for me to get to school.

God provides all for all those who will believe on Him, put Him first, and trust in Him. While I know we live in a very competitive world and God understands our grind, our hustle and bustle, and the need to obtain success and provide for our families, He also wants us to rely on Him. Why not? He is the God of endless possibilities. He is real! He is available to you.

Kings, queens, rulers of large territories, the president of the United States are not people that we have contact with. We as U.S. citizens, have to go through the chain of command in order to get our needs heard and met. We have to go through the proper channels of reaching out to our local mayors and governors to bring attention to community needs. We sometimes have to sign petitions in our local neighborhoods or protest for change.

We are privileged to have the freedoms we have, to present any and all needs before our government officials. How awesome is it that God allows us to pray? We don't have to go through an angel, or through a mayor's office first. As believers in Christ, He gives us full access to His throne at all times, 24/7. Through prayer I can reach out to my heavenly King, instantly. So can you. While access to a king or queen is limited, access to God is instant through birthright. As believers in the rebirth of Jesus Christ, God sees us as sons and daughters just like His very own son Jesus, when we accept Christ as our Savior.

Jesus being the Son of God and of direct royal blood line to God Himself, was the only one who could redeem us back to the Father. Sin had separated us from God in the Garden of Eden. That garden was a perfect paradise. The garden was bountiful, with a large river that divided into four rivers and watered the garden well. Areas of this garden contained gold, pearls and onyx. The garden had *every* tree that is good for fruit growing in it. The birds sang their songs in the fruit trees and the cattle and other animals got along. The beasts were no threat to Adam and Eve.

So Adam and Eve had access to God at all times since God walked through the garden. There was no sickness, disease, crime, no war, no pestilence, no need to work a job, and no evil. But then, Adam and Eve disobeyed God and ate fruit from the tree of knowledge of good and evil. And we have been trying to make it back to paradise ever since.

Look around you, When you put on the television, do you hear president Trump speaking of defending the great Nation of the USA and rumors of possible war? Do you see evidence of crime, disease, hard times, and evil? The earth didn't begin this way. Let's be real, we would love to be back in paradise! Disobedience to God cost Lucifer everything. He is now Satan and he's miserable. Misery loves company. Satan hates us because we still have access to the Father, salvation, prayer, redemption, heaven, healing, peace, joy, eternal life, and he does not. Satan's goal is to confuse us, keep us occupied and busy, deceive us, keep us blind, hidden from truth, so he can kill, destroy and rob our souls from God's loving hands. Let the truth of this book and the bible itself set you free.

The ultimate story of good and evil didn't begin with Superman and Lex Luther. It began in the garden when Adam and Eve disobeyed God and opened the doors for evil to enter the world through eating a forbidden fruit. The knowledge of good *and* evil is now present on this earth and the earth is no longer a paradise.

You see, Adam was the all in one man. Men carry millions of sperm in them. When Adam sinned, the entire human race sinned. Though we were not born yet, all of us were seeds in Adam.

Sin, straight up disobedience to God has serious consequences.

How much mercy can He show us? Let's be real. Have we done anything at all to deserve His mercy, His love, His blessings, and His access to salvation and eternal life? Nothing. We've done nothing at all nor could we ever do anything at all to deserve his benefits. His benefits come through mercy and by obedience as His followers. We follow certain DJs on the radio, we follow those we like on social media, and we follow the Kardashians on TV. Why wouldn't I follow the example of Christ and live my life for God? Do you know anyone else that can offer the benefits of a comforter such as the Holy Spirit to warn you against evil and harm and supply you with the deliverance of eternal damnation? I think not. Let's be real!

CHAPTER 8

Question

I KNOW SOME OF YOU are wondering if God will reveal my own death to me. I'm wondering the same. But for now, I'm enjoying life full-speed ahead. Likewise, I pray that all of you enjoy both life to its fullest and the benefits of knowing our great Creator, both in this life on this earth and beyond.

Psalms 103 in the KJV tells us about God's benefits to mankind. Let's go over some of these benefits, shall we? God forgives us of all wrongdoings. During a lifetime of being so imperfect and facing all kinds of temptations, that may be a lot of wrong doing for some of us. God heals our diseases and supplies us with doctors, surgeons, and nurses to perform the rest. God has supplied those who suffer with arthritis with things like natural anti-inflammatory agents such as ginger, cilantro, turmeric, and cinnamon.

God redeems us from destruction in the sense that we can do nothing at all to redeem ourselves. We are all sinners and we cannot do anything to earn salvation and escape the lake of fire in hell. Only royal blood to the throne of heaven can do that, which would be God's son, Jesus Christ. God is so merciful that He sent His only begotten son to die on the cross in our place. Jesus paid the price for our sinful, fallen nature.

Through Jesus' sacrifice on the cross and resurrection on the third day, He redeemed us back to God the Father so that with believing in Him, accepting Him as your Savior, following His commandments, and denying yourself, we can have access to Him and all His benefits. He did it all for us!

He is a God that satisfies our mouths with good things. Considering that over half the United States is obese, would you say that we've all had a lot of good things to eat? I am included in that for I, myself, was 254 lbs at one time in my life. I am not anywhere near that now. Diet, exercise and disciple, and the right food choices have changed my life. Knowing that God has supplied all that I need, even the foods that I need to restore my body back to health and reduce the inflammation and pain of arthritis through natural anti-inflammatory agents, keeps me in awe of Him.

The Lord also executes righteousness and judgment for those who are oppressed. Would you like access to this God and His benefits? To receive this great Creator and His benefits into your life, you simply need to say this prayer. Repeat after me. *Lord, I believe there is more to life than what I've been living. I confess my sins. I believe you sent your son to die on the cross in my place in order to offer salvation to all those who will accept it. I want to be one of the many that accept your son as Christ, my Savior, and receive access to the Holy Spirit to give me warnings just as you gave Belle many warnings. Lord, please write my name in the Lamb's book of Life and guide my life as I surrender all areas of my life to you, Amen.*

Congratulations! You just made the most important decision of your entire present and future! You are now created by Him, saved by Him, and destined for greatness because of Him!

CHAPTER 9

Deny Myself

To DENY OURSELVES MEANS WE can't normally do all that we want to do. Bummer, I know. This thing called our weak flesh has the desire to do whatever it wants whenever it wants, without discipline of any kind. Jesus on earth did His father's will at all times, not what His own flesh desired. Jesus, knowing His father well and all the benefits His father has to offer, knew better than to fall into temptation. We, too, will be tempted and tested in various ways.

Will you pass the test? It may be difficult when your friends are out there doing their own thing, giving into the pleasures of this world, drinking, smoking, sex with multiple partners, cheating on our spouses, gambling, lying, stealing, etc. We often think it's alright to do the same. If everyone else does it, then why can't we? Well, because there is a cost for all we do. We reap what we sow. If we obey God's commandments and follow Christ's example, we set ourselves up for greatness.

However, if we choose to do what we want all the time, disobeying God's commandments and Christ's example, then we are doomed for the pit of hell. According to my dream in the hospital, while giving birth to Joy, hell is a place I never want to encounter ever. It is far more terrifying than the worst horror movie you've ever seen. The gloomy faces, filled with fear, devastated looks of misery on the highest level, of the long, what seemed never-ending line of people that heard the word of God yet rejected it, were there in my dream.

I'm telling you, the lake of fire is real as the ocean in our world. It appears to be acres long and never ending just like the line of billions of people going into that lake of fire. Don't be one of the ones that goes to hell, into that lake of fire. I saw people shaking so bad that their teeth were shattering right out of their mouths and the flames were hotter than a fiery furnace in a very large crematory.

I do not wish that any of you reach that lake of fire. On the contrary, I wish you to know my God and all of His benefits! He wishes to protect you, bless you, heal you, forgive you, give you the gift of eternal life, and so much more. Won't you allow Him to be the God of your life?

CHAPTER 10

The End Is the Beginning

Now, YOU'RE READY TO START living! Death, where is thy sting? You now belong to the King of kings and Lord of lords. There is no limit to what you can do! Live life to the fullest, put God first at all times, ask God to reveal His audible voice to you and ask Him for protection against the enemy and the spirits of darkness. You are loved. You are now His! Is there any better accomplishment than to belong to your Creator by choice?

Now, go out there and create your own followers of Christ. Spread the good news of God and His benefits. Share your own experiences with others and be a fisher of men. That is to use social media, advertisement, and all means necessary to spread the good news of God to others. What is your story? We all have a story. Who are the Carols, Moms, and Jerry's of your life? What has God delivered you from? Share, post, write, and expose it! I dare you to live for God out loud! I dare you to depend on Him and test Him. He's a good God all the time! He will preserve you as He has preserved me.

Love Belle.

ABOUT THE AUTHOR

I AM AN AVERAGE NEW Yorker that has had some extraordinary experiences. I was born and raised on Long Island which offers beautiful beaches, lots of history, and great people looking to live life to the fullest. That richness in history and lifestyle of taking full advantage of all that life offers is what drew me to be open to the supernatural. We, human beings, all have one thing in common. We all want to be accepted. At the age of fifteen, the acceptance of someone into my life had such a profound effect on me that He changed my destiny. He preserved me to share my story with you. You too may never be the same again!

CPSIA information can be obtained
at www.ICGtesting.com
Printed in the USA
FSHW01n2223240618
49610FS